YOUR COMPI

CANCER 20__

PERSONAL

HOROSCOPE

Monthly Astrological Prediction Forecasts of Zodiac
Astrology Sun Star Sign- Love, Romance, Money, Finances,
Career, Health, Spirituality

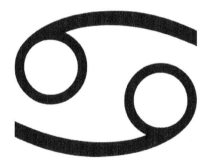

Iris Quinn

Contents

PERSONALITY PROFILE

Constellation: Cancer

Zodiac symbol: Crab

Date: June 20 – July 22

Zodiac element: Water

Zodiac quality: Cardinal

Greatest Compatibility: Taurus and Capricorn

Sign ruler: Moon

Day: Monday and Thursday

Color: White

Birthstone: Ruby

Cancer! Yeah, you saw right. People of this zodiac sign often project themselves into the future through their imagination. They live more in the past and future than the present. They hold on to the past, making it difficult for them to easily let go of grudges and make them resentful and clingy. They care more about their roots- they hold their family and friends dearly. You find many of them getting married very early because their love for family makes them want to start a family of their own as early as possible.

They have a special dedication to children, and they are motherly and sentimental. They love to be around people; loneliness becomes too much for them to bear. They are big dreamers and creative too. They tend to bring innovation and ideas anywhere they are. They are trustworthy, and their loyalty is second to none. They are truthful and reliable.

Moon

The Moon is a feminine planet symbolizing emotions and the subconscious, subtle inner forces and currents. All aspects of family, home and roots are ruled by the Moon, and this planet also has a link to dreams. The Moon is the Sun's polarity, 'yin' in nature and symbolic of femininity, nurturance, empathy, the mother, the subconscious, emotions, passivity, gentleness, receptivity, and instincts. People with a strong Lunar (Moon) placement tend to have very powerful and well-developed instincts. All aspects of inner feelings and desires are connected to the Moon, and wisdom is down-to-earth, mature and grounded; humility and grace combined with a strong feminine energy are the Moon in essence. Cancer is this planet's ruling sign, the 4th house is ruled by the Moon too.

Everything 'hidden' comes under the Moon's realm. Not only are attitudes towards roots, home & family including our foundations are included here, but past experiences and the emotional memories we hold go onto are within this planet's realm. Memories that shape our attitude, behaviors, and beliefs around roots, home and family help to heal our wounds, further helping us to step into the light. Topics of protection, security, sex, primal instincts and survival needs come into focus as well.

Month by Month Forecast

January 2022

Horoscope

There might be a need for Cancer to resolve social issues this January. Your commitments will be under fire, and your strong emotions might be uncontrollable. Perhaps you may want to explain your sentiments concerning your family and partner, but it seems overwhelming.

You will maintain a sense of balance, calmness, peace, and clarity of mind in handling your business and completing projects. However, avoid overindulgence in some of your favorite activities like gambling, drinking liquor, and eating food.

It matters so much that you have self-discipline and self-control. Otherwise, you might see yourself easily triggered and hating the people around you.

Love and Romance

From January 24 to March, three planets will be in Capricorn, Mars, Venus, and Pluto. It connotes that you will experience a tamed love life. Fights with your spouse or partner will lie low, and this month will kick off great for people in long-term relationships.

The month is perfect for soulmates. With trust and respect, you may maintain a harmonious relationship that can strengthen your union.

On the contrary, however, sour relationships can lead to unreciprocated love. The couple will experience hostility, so it is better to let go. The antagonistic stance in your bond can either make your relationship strong or break you apart.

Work and Career

Dedication and persistence will be your ladder to success. The growth in your career may be unexplainable, but your consistency will help you achieve things at work. The first step can be the hardest, but your diligence can produce great results later on.

There may be inequality at work. The instability must not be a stumbling block that will hinder your success. Use it as a challenge and strive harder. Ditch whatever can ruin progress in your career. Do not be affected by the intimidating workspace, and counter the hostility with a warm smile and positive outlook.

Money and Finances

It is an exciting month for Cancer. January 2022 will bring financial stability. You have to be serious with the investments you will make. Use your time in building up your savings and satisfying your obligations.

Maintaining balance is necessary for you to live a comfortable life. Prioritize necessary purchases and utility bills before using your funds for luxurious things. When it comes to the financial condition, you may not be making so much for now, but the investments you are making may bring you good returns in the months to come.

Health and Spirituality

Do things in moderation, Cancer. Your decision to pursue self-improvement is the best step towards your goal to bring balance back into your life. However, you have to commit to a progressive plan that may affect your overall lifestyle.

You have to look for diversity around you to give your spirit a time to connect with nature. An imbalance in your body, mind, and soul can destroy the peace within you. Aim to recharge and refresh from time to time. Out-of-town trips can also be a great escape to prevent burnout.

Your failures in carrying out plans will draw you closer to God. Do not let negativity consume you.

With fervent prayer and communication to our Lord, you can overcome the obstacles in your life.

Horoscope

February showcases defined goals and progress. There will be abundant blessings but some of which are intangible, like love and loyalty. You will savor success this month, and with excellent advice in handling money, you will achieve financial stability.

2022 will introduce a person who will care for you like a mom. She is calm and prowess. Her mere presence can boost your confidence, and her rationality will uplift you and teach you how to restore peace in your family.

Passion is the best part of 2022. By assuming risks, you will gain a competitive edge in your field of work. February is a reminder for you not to be overly controlling. Instead, focus on self-development to reach your desired outcome. With your strong will to succeed, you will find what you need.

Love and Romance

Single Cancer will have the chance to start a romantic bond with someone who keeps them interested. Now is not the time to chase. You have to wait and receive love as it presents itself to you.

You will not be so lucky in relationships, maybe because you will be exhausted chasing your dreams this month. Searching for love is not on your priority list.

As you wait, you can improve your personality and make a careful assessment of yourself. Transform if you have to, and you will slowly realize that there is a lot to improve.

If you are in a long commitment, you may convince your partner that you can build a happy home. You are already close to sealing the deal.

So, wedding bells may soon ring with your gentle charm and genuine loving.

Work and Career

Cancer, by loving yourself you will stand out. You will unnoticeably gain confidence as you pamper your person. With your natural wit and charisma, your colleagues at work will adore you, and they will support you in your endeavors.

Your charm can captivate future business partners. So, you can start an independent venture in a peaceful environment. You will either become a reliable or a responsible woman who will guide you as you establish your business. She can become a partner or a business advisor.

It is unlikely for you to encounter unpleasant things this month. When it comes to working, you will feel comfortable and light. You will perform efficiently in such a peaceful workplace.

Money and Finances

Your money issues will not be as complex as before. The amount you will shed for investments will only be a portion of your savings. Hence, you can be sure that your motherly instinct of saving more than spending will help you provide for your family in the months to come.

Perhaps you will be frugal as soon as your businesses start to operate, and with this strategy in mind, your budget will meet your necessities. By the time your investments yield profit, you will still have more than enough in your pocket. Luxurious assets did not impress you in the past, and despite your fortune now, they still won't.

Health and Spirituality

Welcome a healthier you this month, Cancer. Your mother's care and love will help you strengthen your core and improve your physical stance. There is a chance that you will not heed your vices and practice self-control when eating and staying up late.

You will maintain your shape, and your positivity will be contagious. You will influence the people around you to have an optimistic view of life and get rid of their bad habits. In turn, you will meet a woman who will help you enrich your spirituality.

With her wisdom and kindness, you will search for God, and you will deliberately work and reach out to those in need. You will act in a way that pleases Him.

March 2022

Horoscope

Maturity and success abound Cancer this March. The warm personality that makes you a perfect public servant will exude, and everyone will see your good qualities as a person. You will yearn for personal growth, and you will explore the world to help others.

You tend to focus on material possessions, and it will be enlightening to know that you will soon realize that money has no value. This month, you will happily expand your horizon. Seeing the beauty in things beyond your money will give you peace and comfort.

Love and Romance

Do not dwell too much on your family's problems. You will aim for stability financially. It means they will not be essential to you in the meantime.

In 2022, you will be at the stage of a relationship wherein your partner will view you as a King.

Your dominance, nurturing attitude, loyalty, and power will give your partner a sense of security. Single Cancer must learn how to listen to their inner emotions. Fortunately, you will fall for someone who loves you sincerely.

Married Cancer will find opportunities to welcome a stranger at home. A caveat, do not trust easily. This year, couples must be wary of deceit or dishonesty under their roof.

Work and Career

You will enjoy opportunities that can help your career to flourish. Your energy will be more than enough to sustain a promotion at work, and your excitement will make you do amazing things to prove your worth.

Your career will be in a good stance. An expert in his field may give you insights on how to excel at work. Like a King, this man will gain your trust and confidence because of his wisdom. You will respect him and learn from his teachings.

You are great as a person. But this noble man's help will make you reach your goals earlier than expected. There will be a realization of business plans, and these investments will prosper despite the pandemic.

Money and Finances

Having calculated risks can give you hindsight on what you can achieve with your investments. Be careful, however, in making large purchases. Even if your businesses are doing well, greedy eyes are waiting for your fall. You might get lured to invest in scams involving huge sums.

You may expect a handsome return from your business ventures. With optimism and enthusiasm, you may also have enough to share with those in need. You are innately generous,

Cancer. You will share and care for the people who have less and those who have none.

Health and Spirituality

It is the proper time to focus on your wellness. You should develop good habits that will translate to physical strength and mental clarity. Timely medical intervention when it comes to your health issues may assure you of fast recovery. Free yourself from anxiety and depression.

Discount negative thoughts to improve your overall health. As you focus on filling your bank accounts, you are slowly veering away from our Creator. Keep your faith in God Almighty and know that our earthly treasures are worthless in the afterlife.

April 2022

Horoscope

The past months may have been draining and stressful for you due to family issues. This April, Cancer will experience romantic relationships intensify as Mars and Venus enter Pisces. Past family disputes will slowly fade. The struggles in power and priority at home will not be an issue anymore.

April may mean hardships when it comes to health. It shows a negative omen indicative of exhaustion, adversity, hunger, and suffering. Your frustrations will add more pressure, so learn how to re-energize and refresh so you can win the race.

In April, Cancerians will allow their family and loved ones to take control based on planetary positions.

Love and Romance

There will be changes in your family and relatives' expectations and priorities at home. You will openly discuss things with them to avoid issues again.

Sadly, in terms of love life, you may experience bad luck this month, Cancer. If you are in a relationship, this connotes that you will experience rejection and neglect. On the other hand, your partner will realize how ill-treated they are. Thus, there is a chance for divorce, disgrace, or break-ups.

Personal issues and the demands in your family may affect your career growth. More so, even if you want to devote quality time to your spouse or partner, you will have a hard time doing so.

Thus, arguments may arise, and your love life will undergo crucial times.

Single Cancer need not rush in love. Chances are, love will be unrequited or not worth it.

Work and Career

You are currently overwhelmed by your backlogs at work, and you will realize that this is not the job you want to do for the rest of your life. However, you will be stuck, and there is a slim chance for you to do what you love most.

Cancer might face unemployment issues this April. So, if you feel like leaving your workplace or you want to dodge the tasks you need to do, try to handle it and bear the hardships. Otherwise, you might end up losing your only source of income.

Money and Finances

Your horoscope foretells that you will have a salary increase this month since you hurdled the job through the pandemic. It will be a blessing to have since you will have a stable income despite lockdowns.

The career you have may be quite demanding at this point, but one good thing to note is that your bosses can see your diligence. With your workload, they will gladly offer financial help to provide for your family. Since you have shown loyalty and perseverance, there is a big chance for promotion in the coming months.

Health and Spirituality

Reoccurrence of your old sickness is imminent. So, watch the food you eat, your lifestyle, and your vices. Cancer must commit to better health options. Take care of yourself and improve your wellness by engaging in some relaxing activities like yoga and meditation.

Your struggles in providing financial support to your family are giving your body a hard time too.

It may not show up early, but stress and anxiety can negatively affect your nervous system.

In the spiritual context, you will find people with different views and beliefs. Be open to discuss with them and surround yourself with people who can enrich your faith and spirituality. God sees your efforts, and the more you seek Him, the closer you are to salvation.

Horoscope

The universe will lead you to the right path. It will not be a difficult choice since you have the gifts of wisdom and courage. But then, you will not have an easy win. Not knowing what lies in the future, you will hope to have made the right decision.

As you move on with life, Cancer, someone with power and authority will support you in your career. His knowledge and experience at work will be your guide in times of difficulty.
He is noble and well-respected. His words are powerful, and his charm will make you work with him at ease.

Despite the words of your mentor, you will have the freedom to give the final say. Although it can be scary to decide against his findings, you will be able to end up with a better solution through his helpful insights. In the end, you still have to trust yourself more than anyone else.

Love and Romance

You will be acting like a boss on most days of May. Eager to accomplish many things in your mind, you might be a leader than a follower. With the planet Mars affecting your actions, your high sexual drive and dominance at bed are highly likely. You want to take action, and it is a good thing for you and your partner. Couples might be inseparable this month.

On the contrary, your relatives may feel unease with the strong words you may utter, and you will fail to notice this. They may hold grudges, and there can be misunderstandings. Something will happen that will make you shift 360 degrees from being an authoritative leader to a listener.
For singles, you will decide between your suitors.

With your busy schedule this year, you will also consider committing. If you get to meet someone who can appease your heart despite lack of time, Cancer will surely keep them.

Work and Career

There will be a success in all of your career pursuits. Cancer will encounter challenges at work. With sufficient preparation and knowledge, you can resolve these issues.

You will continue learning. Perhaps you will spend on books and subscribing to webinars and online classes. As your focus on self-improvement, you will feed your academic thirst to be a deserving boss. Your workmates will see your efforts, and they will trust you even more. You will delight yourself in God's ways, and He will help you through your life.

Conflicts at work will make you feel torn between friends, and you will resolve the same without considering closeness and loyalty. You may lose a friend because of issues on betrayal and impartiality.

Money and Finances

Cancer, you will receive a hefty amount this May. The Sun will help you improve your income, and this may result in yielding more. There will be opportunities to grab, and among these is the strategy to make your income exceed your expenses.

You will make savings a natural thing. More of a regular habit, you will allocate an amount for necessary expenses and keep much of your income for an emergency. You must limit spending on things you need than those you want, and it will help you attain financial stability easily.

You will need money for investing, and with this simple strategy, you may enjoy a comfortable life while your savings grow continuously.

Health and Spirituality

2022 is not a positive year for you, Cancer. Saturn may negatively affect your health except in June to September. You may be very sensitive to diseases, so you have to be cautious about getting ill.

It seems that you are aiming to lose weight by eating a balanced diet. You are on the right track as long as you will do it while considering the effects on your body. You have to avoid bottling up strong emotions. This practice may give you heart ailments later in life.

In the context of spirituality, you will focus on enriching spiritual consciousness. The Lord God will be pleased with your growth in faith and love for your fellow.

Horoscope

From May to October, you will have to deal with some complicated issues. Minor issues will arise, and it will lead to arguments at work.

Make peace with your colleagues, and things will become smooth in your career. Jupiter will affect your social life this 2022. There will be great opportunities for you to build networks and meet new friends.

From June to October, Jupiter will be in Aries. It means you might be working with the wrong crowd. Neptune in Pisces connotes that you may attract people with the same interests, and you will be spending time for hobbies and public events together.

June will be peaceful, and it promises a lot of personal revelations and a genuine desire to share with others.

Love and Romance

It can be a tricky month for you. You will feel great, but your health is compromised, and you will not notice the changes. Take care of yourself, so you can also have the chance to care for those you love.

The second half of 2022 shows a pattern of calm and serenity. When Mars enters Taurus in June and Venus enters Scorpio in September, comfort, and harmony will fill the air.

It is a perfect month for a sensual dinner. You may expect romance until the end of the year. So, shake your life up and make memories to cherish. Love with intimacy may lead to engagement, marriage, or pregnancy.

If you are single, this month may encourage new love or happiness with friends. You will strengthen the bond you have with people, and it will make your life lighter than before.

Work and Career

You may expect partnerships at work or network building for your career progress. You will reach farther, and you will empower yourself by giving more than receiving. You will be in a state of stability in your career that can help others with what you make.

There will be good working terms with the company, so the possibility of promotion and salary increase is a goal to keep.

If you are still looking for a job, with patience and perseverance, you will be employed before the month ends, and you will have the chance to provide a comfortable life for your family.

Money and Finances

Deception may get you a job but be careful since lies will always be out in the open, in time. Apply for work that requires the skills you have.

Pretending to be qualified to have a lucrative job will help you secure a job, but maintaining will be a big challenge.

You can learn new things fast, so take this as an advantage. Save your earnings to build the dream house you have been planning to have for years. Be reminded that illegal means is never an option to provide a quality life for your family.

Health and Spirituality

June shows a positive stance in terms of health. You will regain strength if you start early. Avoid engaging in harmful practices and study your family's medical history to know your vulnerability.

You have to avoid risky situations as you are prone to accidents this month. Cancer, you may become ill with an environmentally triggered disease.

When it comes to spirituality, your family will start a generation that is more entwined with religion. A solid connection and foundation centered on Jesus, our redeemer. You will receive more blessings, and your house will be open to people who need help. Consider yourself lucky, Cancer.

July 2022

Horoscope

Cancer will create more revenue after June, which will be useful in the coming years. Do not waste your money on useless items because 2022 will provide you with the opportunity to earn.

Invest in your academic interests while also doing your best to keep track of your finances. Hobbies that are within your financial means are not a bad thing. Cancerians are vivacious, and you may have fun while keeping your wallet full.

To avoid disagreements with others, try to freely express your objectives and views. Your dating skills may be outmoded, but your special someone will value your amorous intentions over your deeds.

Love and Romance

You may give love a new meaning if you want to. It's great news for couples because you'll be able to nourish and strengthen your bond. You will devote time to personal pleasures, which will make your life partner pleased.

Spend some time pampering yourself at a spa or a massage clinic. Work and home life will be a little more tough in July 2022. So, put your priorities first and focus your efforts on the things that count.

This year, people who have just broken up will find a more stable commitment in their lives. You'll finally understand why the past never worked. Fortunately, your new love will be there for you no matter what.

Work and Career

Young Cancer will be pleased because you may be granted scholarship sponsors as well as a promising professional route. You'll get high-paying positions, and you'll be able to refine your management skills to become an effective boss.

Starting a business is also something you enjoy. As a result, doing business and trading will assist you in becoming affluent. It is feasible for you to achieve financial success. Enjoy your uncertain and modest life for the time being.
Your skills will serve you well throughout your life, but it will be your prudent investments that will bear fruit in the future.

Money and Finances

There will be a lot of learning, and your buddies will be your best ally. Their support will help you improve your attitude and work successfully because you are naturally emotional and bashful.

However, be cautious because your sensitivity may interfere with your ability to concentrate at work. So long as you don't let your bad emotions get in the way, you'll amaze your superiors with your devotion and constancy. You will be able to support your family if you give up your laid-back attitude.

Health and Spirituality

Getting the correct eating plan and fitness programme might help you achieve your health goals. You can get healthy in the long run if you practice self-discipline. You are possessive, and your clingy attitude will prevent you from focusing on yourself. Try to get rid of this personality because it can have a negative impact on your mental health.

When it comes to spirituality, your zeal will aid you in gaining knowledge. Your spiritual gifts will assist you in identifying persons who can motivate you to improve and strengthen your relationship with God.

Achieving our life objectives is a blessing, but helping others achieve their aspirations is a way for us to be successful in spirit.

August 2022

Horoscope

You'll automatically gain confidence this month since you're feeling fortunate, which you are. Work is enjoyable, and you will motivate your coworkers to be productive.

August marks the beginning of the year-long process of putting money aside for rainy days. You will learn how to handle your finances efficiently after a thorough examination of your sources of income. You are willing to try new ways to get money, and you will be successful in these endeavors.

You should be prepared for a prospective proposal or a deeper degree of commitment shortly after August 26th, 2022. Even in public, love and romance will be visible, and your lover will appreciate it.

Love and Romance

August is the greatest month to go on a trip with your friends and family. A fantastic trip for rekindling old passions and bridging two hearts. For Single Cancer, expect to see the beginning of a commitment.

Even if a relationship isn't on your mind, the sincerity with which your suitor loves you will astound you. Be truthful to yourself. In any case, there is no such thing as a perfect time to fall in love.

For couples, this may imply marriage or the birth of a child. Yes, your love will allow you to start a family. Give yourself some time to recharge and re-energize for more adventure in the following days, for your optimism will be your ladder success.

You can expect to be in a great mood for the majority of the days. You'll radiate joy, and your humility will inspire others to put their faith in you. Your candor will cause your colleagues to display their true colors as well.

Work and Career

You require work in order to survive. It's comforting to know that you'll figure out how to achieve your goals. You can support your family's needs for a living if you enjoy what you do. You might be astonished to learn that your hard work on the job will not go unnoticed.

It helps if you recognize the importance of stepping up and proving your worth at work. This mindset will assist you in reaching the pinnacle. You'll show self-discipline in your work, and your bosses will reward you with perks like free international trips.
Your confidence and self-esteem will be boosted as a result of the opportunities provided by your job. You will decide to read more and learn more.

Money and Finances

Spending money on yourself is a worthwhile investment. Don't be too hard on yourself because you worked hard. You are deserving of a pleasant treat, whether it be a trip or a meal.

Learn to keep a firm grip on your money, even if it isn't a pandemic. Extend your revenue and eliminate wasteful spending. The secret to living a comfortable life is to plan ahead.

In light of the COVID outbreak, you might want to consider signing up for a sideline through an online platform. Freelancing is a great way to supplement your income. It is, however, if you know how to self-discipline and work with minimal supervision.

Health and Spirituality

You've entered a period of tension in your life. Regardless of the benefits you receive from your job, remember to keep your immune system under check. Stress may wreak havoc on your health, putting you vulnerable to disease.

Try to maintain a good exercise routine and a well-balanced diet, just as you did at the start of the year. Another important aspect that you have overlooked is sleep. Make sure you get enough sleep on a daily basis.

You'll be in constant communication with the universe. You'll discover how to use prayer to access the spiritual realm, as well as how to incorporate the Bible and its gospels into your daily life. Your relationship with Jesus will provide you with peace and security.

Horoscope

You will be prone to experience irascibility and pressure for the entire September. You may become a bit insomniac, and it will be uncomfortable for you to enjoy family events in the morning.

Nevertheless, you will meet new friends who will be your support group in the years to come. They will be reliable, and they will help you appreciate ME-time or time for your refreshment.

Do not let your tedious work take a toll on your health. The effect can be irreversible. Try to reduce stress and anxiety by performing your tasks one day at a time, and you will be able to get past the hard part with composure.

Love and Romance

The old saying is correct, devote your time to your family to enjoy life and not waste it. Work needs you, but once you are gone, they can easily find someone to replace you. It is not the same with family.

September will bring renewed strength, and you should fight against the stress your projects may cause you. This month can be a good excuse for you to spend some time with your partner, away from your laptop and to-do list.

Singles must not only use their hearts this time. The mind must work before considering marriage. On the other hand, couples may take pleasure in the giggles of a newborn since pregnancy is possible.

Work and Career

You have a fulfilling job, and if you are considering academic pursuit, your chances are impressive. Success, fortune, and stability await you in terms of your professional career.

Your willingness to finish your course will make it possible for you to carry out your plans. As you work, you will juggle your time with reading and studying. You will try to make a routine you can follow for the entire year. 2022 is a fruitful year for you, Cancer.

Money and Finances

Although it is tempting to spend on things you love, avoid buying impulsively. Your financial status is starting to be stable, do not ruin what you have banked on. Learn to take account of everything, so you will know where every penny goes.

Your excellent work ethic will give you a chance to receive a salary increase or monetary reward from your bosses. Thus, if your budget is tight, you have additional funds to make ends meet.

Your dedication to serving the company will give you an edge over your other colleagues. You can reach milestones that lead to better opportunities in your career.

Health and Spirituality

Being too preoccupied is your number one (1) enemy. The stress your work brings can threaten your health or worsen existing illnesses.

Browse through the internet for some helpful tips in taking care of yourself. Since your job requires you to stay in front of the desk most of the time, try to include exercise in your daily tasks. It will help you avoid a sedentary lifestyle that can lead to the development of illnesses.

Your connection to the world seems to overcome your communication with the spiritual realm.

Deliberately try to talk to God every day, and he will help you maintain balance in your hectic lifestyle.

October 2022

Horoscope

Cancer, you're going to be in charge this month. Someone will assist you with legal issues, and you will be confident in what you have learnt. Do not think of yourself as superior to others. Be confident in your ability to do good rather than causing controversy or discouragement.

In October, it's likely that you'll be assisting others in winning their struggles. Despite the fact that you are not a party to the dispute, you will assist someone who is uneducated. Knowing they can't defend themselves, you're willing to step in and help them solve the problem in a just and equitable way.

Keep in mind not to become too engrossed in the difficulties. Maintain a cool demeanor when listening and speaking.

Love and Romance

You can be uncomfortable with your partner. It's possible that your connections will proceed slowly, but be patient. The wait will be worthwhile. Socialize and avoid erecting barriers around yourself. With your pals, you will grow slowly.

Singles may encounter someone with a severe demeanor, firm convictions, and strong convictions. They will, thankfully, develop strong feelings for you. They may be appealing to you as potential companions. As a result, there's no reason for you to be hesitant. They genuinely want to learn more about you.
However, if you are a dominant personality, especially if you are a Cancer lady, learn to listen and follow.

Work and Career

Despite the lack of recognition, this is an excellent time to focus on projects and put in effort. Not everyone will treat you the same way the rest of the world does. Your superiors may be strict, but they will think about your acts even if they don't tell you about them.

If you're a single Cancer, you might encounter someone who makes you uncomfortable at work. A person with an authoritarian personality will act in ways that you dislike. Keep a close eye on him and enjoy his small actions. You might mistake him for someone he isn't only because of his unconventional approach to things.

Money and Finances

When it comes to your money troubles, be practical. There are some things you need to acquire and expenses to pay that take precedence over other important activities on your to-do list.

You need to figure out how to save more money than you spend. Limit your generosity to a portion that you can provide without causing hardship to your family. To be honest, you might get monetary benefits as a reward.

Health and Spirituality

Some signs can cause your present health state to be misdiagnosed. Make the decision to be open and honest with your doctor. Don't be embarrassed to talk about what's bothering you. Give him as much information as possible about your health concerns.

Every ailment has its own set of treatment options, so you'll need a better grasp of your situation before you can seek the right treatment. Miracles do happen, and you can petition God for healing if you have confidence and trust in Him.

November 2022

Horoscope

The rest of the year will be smooth, and all the problems you have encountered will be part of the past. You do not have to dwell on things that will not help you bounce back. Put your sentiments aside and choose to put your energy into rebuilding yourself.

You will become more confident, happy, and active. This November, things will work out for your good, and it will help set your mood for the months to come. You are going to meet someone who will patiently support you in your goal to succeed.

Love and Romance

Cheating can happen anytime, but make sure not to give in to violence, abuse, intimidation, or any form of retaliation. Your love life will be stable this month, but your plan to get back to your old life might make you too busy over other matters than your partner. Lack of quality time can lead to arguments or break-ups.

Your heart is not prepared to deal with sensitive issues. Heated arguments can trigger you to inflict harm to others. Nevertheless, remember that although you got hurt in the past, God can restore you.

Be mindful of your family's safety and draw strength from your kids. Your mind needs rest, so give it some time to breathe.

Work and Career

This November, you will have sufficient energy to obtain professional success, Cancer.

You are eager to finish a lot of work, and you can be productive when you use strategies that can expedite your tasks. Your commitment to carry our projects will matter at work. Your seniors will ask for help due to the pressure and hostility in your workplace.

It will be fast-paced, and relaxation might not be a good thing to consider for now. Work will be your loathing for your partner, but despite negativity at work, you will be persistent.

Money and Finances

View things lightly and be optimistic. Stress can only bring your negative emotions; so be careful of the friends you choose to stay around. Your career is on the right track, and your finances will be stable, thanks to the investments you have made early on.

Try to be liquid whenever possible. You need to settle your obligations in cash, so always keep an amount in your bank account to cover your bills. You will have a fruitful 2022, so be kind to yourself.

Health and Spirituality

Make it a point not to miss your health check-ups. The pressure of your work and the anxiety you may experience from a nagging partner can affect your mental health big time. Prioritize your health in the earliest possible chance.

Rest if you have to. Eat whatever your body needs and take some time off your hectic schedule to relax and free your mind from all the struggles in your life this month.

Your emotional challenges are nothing with God. So come to Him and air your sentiments directly. His heart is kind and pure, and he is waiting for you. He may grant you wisdom, strength, and peace if you will call upon Him and stay in His embrace.

December 2022

Horoscope

There will be a total Solar eclipse in December, and it can signify more work with bonuses and rewards. The month may bring passionate and romantic moments for lovers and pure bliss even to those who are still courting their special someone.

Openness, laughter, and peace will be a gift to you this month, Cancer. Although you will encounter issues at work, you will be able to foster peace and camaraderie among your colleagues. With such optimism, you can bounce back from failures with renewed strength and honed skills.

Love and Romance

Harmonious relationships may end up as a permanent union. If you have been in an intimate relationship that respects, trusts, and loves, then you are in for a long-term one.

Single Cancer may find their soulmate this time, but it will not guarantee a tightly bonded love. Fleeting love affairs are possible for you.

If you are a Cancer man, you will enjoy the burning passion of your love towards someone who reciprocates it with the same intensity or even more. You are bound to meet the person with tender love and faithfulness for you.

Cancer women may find a career to be essential than a lasting relationship. But once in love, they can commit without getting too entangled with their lovers. Freedom without a pinch of jealousy is what she can offer.

Work and Career

December 2022 is the end of the year, and you will find yourself getting devoted to your career growth. There can be efforts to reach your plans of becoming successful in a slow-paced and well thought of strategy.

You will grow tired and confused. But despite being overworked, you will try not to make even a single mistake. Sorting out realizable goals and ditching toxic people who may prevent you from reaching your dream will be your resolution for next year. You will start ironing out your plans by the end of the month.

Money and Finances

Do not let anyone stop you from your financial goals. Aim high and do not be affected by silent competition. You have to fight for your right to make a living. Do this, and your promotion will help you gain higher pay and benefits.

Surrender your plans to God and keep your moral values intact. Eventually, someone will help you discover how to make things easier in life, and you will be excited to hold on to the promise of providence in the years ahead.

You may end up establishing a company that will not only benefit you financially. Your ideas will make you big, and popularity is possible in your field of interest next year.

Financial struggles will help you learn a few quick tips to handle your money and make ends meet.

Health and Spirituality

You are planning to solve your issues on weight, and your plan to go to the gym or have a regular swimming session can be a good strategy. As early as now, be mindful of what you eat and practice portion control.

Take action and try not to overindulge in food to lessen your issues as regards weight. Focus on getting the nutrition you want and not on making your physique fabulous, as it will happen by course.

Aside from your family, you will receive tremendous support from your Bible group. Your failures in life will help you meet the kind of people you need, and you will be able to find the path to our savior Jesus Christ. Indeed, he is close even when your heart is in sorrow.

Printed in Great Britain
by Amazon

72092080R00037